Wisdom In Work Clothes

25 Quotes to Provide Wisdom for the Work Place
VOLUME ONE

By
Kwame S. Salter
And Twenty-five Wise Work Place Owls

Copyright @ Kwame S. Salter, 2023

Printed in the United States of America
Published by:
The Salter Group LLC

Janice Fenn, Editor

Cover concept: Janice Fenn
Book design: Patricia Rasch

All rights reserved. No part of this book may be reproduced or transmitted in any form or by any means, graphic, electronic, or mechanical, including photocopying, recording, taping, or by any information storage or retrieval system, without the permission in writing from the author.

For licensing/copyright information, for additional copies or for use in specialized settings contact:

Kwame S. Salter
thesaltergroupllc@gmail.com

ISBN: 979-8-218-15604-6

Acknowledgement

The idea for writing this little book came from Mark White, a former protégé and still valued friend. Mark and I worked together at Oscar Mayer and later Kraft Foods. Mark is a brilliant, passionate, and insightful observer of human behavior, and we have stayed in contact over the years.

I too am a keen observer and evaluator of human behavior. I frequently share my insights as personal quotes, or quotes I've curated from others. After posting several of my quote-filled observations on the very popular LinkedIn site, Mark, also an aficionado of a powerful and timely quote, encouraged me to compile a collection of my more memorable quotes and observations. Mark's vision for this book is that it should be a short book for people in the business world. His advice was to write a book that "young professionals and the still hungry and engaged seasoned professionals could benefit from and use."

I would be remiss not to give a shout-out to Janice Fenn. Janice is my amazing editor and business associate. Her contribution to this work is under the section entitled "Workplace Application." Janice draws on her decades of Corporate and consultant experience with Fortune 500 companies. Janice's superpower is her ability to reduce the complex jargon of business to simple and clear insights. I consider her contributions to this book a bonus for the readers.

I am forever indebted to Mark for his inspiration and to Janice for her relentless determination to see this little book completed. We hope you enjoy and benefit from this first volume.

Prologue

Quotes have always intrigued me! To many, quotes are just trite and clever little sayings that are easy to remember. To me, a good quote represents the distillation of wisdom down to its essential meaning. They communicate profound truths and life applications. I use them frequently, both my own pearls of wisdom and those of others, in my written and spoken communications.

In today's world, we are inundated by a blizzard of information on how to improve ourselves, both personally and professionally. Much of this information comes to us as academic research papers, blog posts, books, magazine articles and on-line videos. The challenge is to extract from each of these outlets the information that is both relevant and useful.

The advantage of using quotes to convey insights is that they are high definition snapshots of wisdom from people who have learned something from their life experiences. Each quote in this book is reality tested. The lesson to be learned is clear, not buried under a cascade of ten-dollar words. A great quote does not require that we crack a secret code to glean the important insights. Consider, for instance, this short quote:

"But remember, a dream doesn't become reality through magic; it takes sweat, determination and hard work."
Colin Powell

This quote is beautiful in its simplicity, wisdom, insightfulness, and memorability. In this book, we present even more wise and memorable quotes. In fact, there are 25 amazing quotes curated to lead you to a new level of workplace wisdom. So, get ready to grasp these extraordinary insights, then work diligently to embrace them as they guide you to experience triumphs beyond your most inspired dreams. Wisdom, put into action, spells "Success!'

1

> "The Truth will set you free. But first, it will piss you off!"
> – Gloria Steinem

It doesn't matter how mentally strong or sure we are about the rightness of our point of view, truthful feedback is hard to swallow. Even if the feedback is unequivocally true, we wince, make a face, or react angrily. Deep in our objective consciousness, we know what we heard was the truth. Still, it's difficult to move off of a position or perspective that we have nurtured and refined over a long period. Yet, to avoid being "stuck on stupid", we need to remain open to both the facts and realities that challenge our long-held presumptions. To become a free thinker requires that we remain open to the fact that, "If we're not careful, we might learn something."

Workplace Application

L-I-S-T-E-N to feedback! Not only the feedback that is provided to you, but listen to the critiques being offered about others. Even if the motive for the feedback is not honorable, evaluate to see if there is any truth from which you may benefit. Then, without further ado, shift!

2

> *"If you think you can do a thing or think you can't do a thing, you're right."*
> – Henry Ford

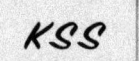

Your mind can be a powerful ally or enemy. Believing in yourself, your ability and your vision will propel you to great heights. While positive thoughts are necessary for achieving anything, you must back up these positive thoughts with preparation, skill, and ability. Without a positive belief in yourself, all the preparation, skill and ability are for naught. We form our thoughts and thus our thinking through 'self-talk' or internal dialogue. Begin taking control of your internal dialogue. The first voice we hear in the morning and the last voice we hear before sleep come from our thoughts. If we are continually telling ourselves that we can't, then we won't! When a negative thought appears, trump it with a positive thought. Figure out what you need to do to achieve your objectives, then "Just do it." Move beyond positive affirmations to positive and productive behaviors.

Workplace Application

It's proven that our thoughts and feelings determine our behaviors. Thus, the key is to change what you think and how you feel — about you primarily! Pick a date for you to shift negative thinking and non-productive feelings (especially feelings of low self-esteem and "woe is me!"). Do the self-talk and practice self-affirmation as you lead up to this date. Remind yourself that you can accomplish every task successfully by taking it step by step. Then, on the set date, begin practicing the new you. Shut down all negative talk from you and others (about you and about others). There is no need for a class, a certificate, or even permission! Just quietly change your outlook to one that is positive! You'll have failures, but if you're truly committed to minimizing negative thoughts and feelings, the successful stretches will become longer and longer, your confidence will grow stronger and stronger, and your turnaround in the organization will become more and more apparent.

> *"Attitude determines the altitude of life."*
> — Edwin Louis Cole

3

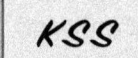

Regardless of the unique talents or smarts you possess, your attitude will either function as gravity to keep you earth bound—or a powerful thrust that will propel you to the heights you aspire to reach in your life. We all have encountered the smart ass who is technically competent but rubs everyone the wrong way. These individuals are demeaning and dismissive towards those they believe to be inferior to them. They make snide remarks about people's intelligence. They are poor listeners and are cynical about human nature. These "demeanors" create 'noise' wherever they land in the organization. Over time, the organization decides that, regardless of their technical ability, their negative attitude is not worth the conflict and complexity they generate. Their fellow employees would rather work alongside a competent person with a positive attitude—versus an exceptionally talented person with a negative spirit. So, if you want to soar in your career, check your negative attitude at the door.

Workplace Application

If you have a negative attitude, no one has to tell you. You already know it! Despite the adverse responses that you receive from co-workers, the burning need to feed your ego by demeaning others trumps all! But — it's a short "high!" Ten minutes after your smart comment or smirk, you're back to being lonely and not well liked, of which you are keenly aware! People tolerate you but don't like you. Pause and consider that you are not obligated to continue in this path. Reset & begin anew. Smile genuinely! Speak pleasant and genuine greetings to your peers and managers. Even if you believe you know the answer, don't be a "know it all." If someone makes a mistake, assist him or her with an attitude of genuine helpfulness. Speak ill of no one. Yes, initially, many will be skeptical of your motives. But by demonstrating consistent genuine and kind behavior, over time you'll find that the "high" you receive from your positive relationships far exceeds the fleeting moments of superiority experienced from your negative behaviors of the past.

> *"A champion is afraid of losing." Everyone else is afraid of winning."*
>
> – Billie Jean King

4

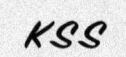

"Play to Win!" Every email I sent as a VP ended with that phrase. Why, you might ask? Well, the answer is obvious. Any game, contest, or career is likely to be forfeited if we are overly cautious. In the business world, 'analysis paralysis' describes the behavior of someone who overthinks a situation with the futile hope of anticipating every potential variable. Unfortunately, real world dynamics don't wait for you to gather all the facts. In reality, there are just too many facts to gather/analyze. The so-called 'facts' are mercurial and subject to change based on real world disturbances. So, those who rationalize their hesitation to act based on the need for further analysis simply get left in the dust. Successful people have an 'unction for action' and know that playing not to lose is not the same as playing to win!

Workplace Application

For most of you reading this book, this is not your first rodeo. You don't have the time and others don't have the patience for you to gather every minute detail before taking action. However, because you know, or should know, what others expect of you, the resources and information at your disposal and the risks that are lurking, you have everything you need to make a sound decision and move forward. So, study the situation at hand; check with key players and subject-matter experts; build a plan; garner strategic support and LAUNCH! Dithering is not an impressive leadership trait.

> *5*
>
> *"You cannot control what happens to you, but you can control your attitude toward what happens to you, and in that, you will be mastering change rather than allowing it to master you."*
>
> *– Brian Tracy*

KSS

Sometimes, you don't get the breaks, the benefit of the doubt, or find yourself in the best situation. You get what you get! However, how you respond to what happens to you is the determining factor. You can resign yourself to the reality of your situation or you can commit to changing that reality. Either decision will require effort. Yet, doing nothing and accepting your fate means that you will expend both mental and emotional energy. Playing the victim is stressful. Victims spend energy simply to survive. Regardless of the amount of victim energy spent, it will not change your situation or your reality. A commitment to changing your situation generates a different type of energy—a self-renewing and bolstering energy!

Workplace Application

Jeff Howard, a Harvard-trained social psychologist and founder of J. Howard & Associates (acquired by Korn Ferry), had as the theme for his enormously popular Efficacy Training program, "It's not the stimulus; It's the response!" His team reinforced to participants that it is not what happens to you (the stimulus) that leads to success or failure, it's the response (what you do as a result). Certainly, there are decisions, circumstances, deeds, and events in the workplace that may be devastating to the psyche, but you don't have to let everyone know how it's affecting you. If something egregious occurs at work, learn to keep your poise. Go home, scream, cry, rant, and threaten. After you're sane again formulate a strategy to move forward. Don't let them see you sweat! If you do, peers will snicker, managers will lose respect, and even some former friends will engage in turning up the temperature in the sauna.

6 · "There are no menial jobs, only menial attitudes."
– William John Bennett

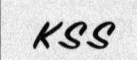

Ever watch a janitor who takes pride in cleaning his/her building, making sure the floors are glistening, the bathrooms are clean and smell good, and the chrome is polished? Too often, we are so enamored with ourselves and our 'big important' job that we barely take notice of the person doing their menial job (by our standards)—with dignity and pride. The lesson that these hard-working people teach us is that it is not necessarily what we do in life—rather, it is how we do it, particularly when we are being paid to do so. I have seen many 'suits' with a big job (and title) bring the most menial attitude to their tasks.

Workplace Application

A former boss shared with me how he amassed so much power that it catapulted him all the way to senior executive. He amassed power by following the advice of a mentor who said, "Never be afraid of accepting a crappy job." He took this to heart and accepted all the functions that no one else wanted. However, he didn't just accept these roles, he strategized, reorganized, and elevated each role, transforming it into a well-respected function. One by one, he re-envisioned and effectuated change to a function that peers suddenly desired.

His boss was stunned to realize one day that he had amassed and was leading a third of the empire! So, the next time the organization offers you a less than favorable role, ACCEPT IT! But don't just accept it, ELEVATE IT significantly. Then, after you've transformed that assignment, prepare to move on and elevate the next assignment!

7

> *"Haters are confused admirers who can't understand why everybody else likes you."*
> – Paulo Coelho

KSS

Regardless of how well we treat people, there will always be some who, for whatever reason, will resent your popularity. Deep in their hearts, these detractors know you are genuine and helpful to all. Yet, they still believe that their role is to point out that you're unworthy of all the admiration/accolades you're getting. In reality, these 'haters' keep you on your toes. Haters believe withholding their admiration will force you to respect them — even when you consistently show them respect. Focusing on the hater is like receiving a standing ovation yet fixating on the one person who refuses to stand. Always remember that haters are nothing more than confused admirers.

Workplace Application

In the workplace, haters are those who attempt to force you to become as mediocre as they are. You strive for excellence, while the haters' motto is "do enough to get by, but with flare." You will go the extra mile, while the haters believe that the road to success stopped exactly where they did – the extra mile doesn't exist! You are diligent in demonstrating integrity and honesty. Their adage is "lie, lie, deny, deny!" In a side-by-side comparison, the distinction is unmistakable and indefensible, the fact of which the haters are keenly aware! Since the haters are unwilling to change, their only recourse is to force you into "living down" to their standards. However, you are much too confident, savvy, and committed to excellence to allow mediocrity to rule the day. So, to your haters, be kind; be gracious; be helpful; and become the personification of the gospel song, "I Shall Not Be Moved!"

> **8** *"I have never developed indigestion from eating my own words."*
> – Winston Churchill

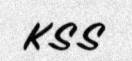

Hubris, excessive pride or arrogance, often leads one to think everything they say is gospel. Even after being shown that what they said was wrong, certain individuals find it hard to admit their mistake. They debate, insult, and even attempt to demean others when challenged. They would rather choke on their misbegotten words rather than eat them. The key to maintaining credibility and authenticity is to admit we've erred and were simply wrong! In fact, eating our own words can be nourishing and beneficial to our professional and personal growth.

Workplace Application

Building credibility is such a long and arduous process, yet one instance of workplace arrogance can destroy it. Conversely, it strengthens your credibility, even when you err, if you handle the situation in the spirit of honesty and humility! Consider that you have built a strong reputation in a particular area. You are called to a meeting where someone questions the data you've provided. Which reaction do you believe will enhance/detract from your credibility? (A) "I'm looking at the data, and you are absolutely correct. I'm really sorry, it's my mistake. I'll get you the correct information." Or, (B) "I've been doing this work for the past 3 years and I've never submitted incorrect data. It was correct when it left my desk. Let me investigate to find out how the error occurred." Response (A) demonstrates that you have the confidence and the integrity to admit that you've made an error. In most cases, your credibility is likely to be further enhanced. In scenario (B), when those involved discover that the error lies with you - and they will because others will not take the blame for your mistake, I'll leave it to you to decide which direction the needle on your credibility meter will move.

9

"If you have a talent, use it in every way possible. Don't hoard it. Don't dole it out like a miser. Spend it lavishly, like a millionaire intent on going broke."

– Brendan Francis

KSS

Too many folks hide their talent. They wait for the right audience, the right opportunity and the right venue to showcase their talent. This is a huge mistake. Instead of aiding a subordinate, a peer or an external customer, they wait until someone they deem 'important' is around to show off their talent. The organization will vet their talent using a 360-degree feedback process that will include their subordinates, boss and peers. To become a genuine star at work means that you make everyone around you better because of your talent. Avoid becoming supercilious and only showing your talent to the top of the organization. The word will get around quickly that your drum only beats to the tune of a highly regarded leader.

Workplace Application

The best opportunity to ensure that others notice your talent is to share it generously and graciously with all, not just with your boss. How your peers feel about your contributions influences how others perceive you to a great extent. You're talented, but do you support your team with your talent, even when you're not asked? Do you give even when you expect nothing in return? Do you offer helpful suggestions to your peers when appropriate? When leaders observe you are a generous team player, they are more likely to form a positive impression about you, and desire to have you on their team. "Give, and it shall be given unto you."

Section Two
Exhibiting Workplace Wisdom Through
ATTITUDE & FORTITUDE

10 — "You tell your mind to run past stop."

— Camryn Salter, My granddaughter

KSS

Each of my children and grandchildren are uniquely talented and gifted. Camryn, my oldest grandchild, is a hard worker and dedicated to excellence in all pursuits. As a middle school student, she took part in cross-country and distance running in track. During a citywide track meet, her relay team was far behind and she was the second to last runner to get the baton. Amazingly, upon receiving the baton, she ran at sprinter speed and closed the gap, bringing her team neck and neck with the leading team as she handed off the baton. Her teammate outran the lead team's closing runner, and they won the race. I was, of course, proud. I was awed by her stamina and speed over such a long distance. After the race, I asked her how she could keep up such an intense pace without getting tired. She responded, simply, "your body wants to stop, but you must tell your mind to run past stop." Every day, our bodies tell us to stop.

Workplace Application

We encounter "Stop Signs" every day, especially in the workplace. Someone receives the promotion that should have been yours. STOP SIGN! Your workload is heavier than your peers. STOP SIGN! You are tired. STOP SIGN! Your boss isn't respectful toward you. STOP SIGN! If you perceive every situation that is not favorable toward you as a STOP SIGN, you've eliminated the possibility of surviving - forget about succeeding. Your career trajectory will be comparable to driving on an interstate that has 4-way stops every 10 miles. If you want to move forward and really succeed, do as Camryn did, "Run Past Stop!"

> **"You will find the key to success under the alarm clock."**
>
> – Benjamin Franklin

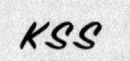

So many people think that success is based on factors like a pleasant personality, the right connections and technical competency alone. While these factors are important, they are not sufficient. First, you must develop the discipline of getting out of bed, just as old Ben Franklin pointed out. Being habitually late for work and meetings is a career killer, and inexcusable if the reason for your tardiness is exhaustion from non-work-related obligations like dating, parties, late night TV and/or social media.

Workplace Application

Get to bed on time so that you can get to work ahead of time. When you arrive at work early, don't waste the time you've gained to "get settled in." You know, getting breakfast and coffee, making the morning rounds of "Hellos" and "Good Mornings," grooming in the restroom. Get to work early and begin work early! Consider the trade-off, 15 to 30 minutes less in the bed for the attainment of a more powerful work ethic that others will observe, admire, and reward.

> *"After all is said and done, usually more is said than done."*
> – Lou Holz,
>   Hall of Fame Football Coach

12

Too often, we are mesmerized by the prose created to address a pressing situation. We address serious situations with old clichés, pious proclamations and public relations strategies. These statements are little more than 'word salads' intended to buy time and not deal with the issue(s) at hand. While we've filled the airwaves with words, somehow we left the actions needed to address the situation on the editing table. Words without accompanying action steps are simply empty calories. This "word salad" needs protein and some high-calorie dressing.

Workplace Application

How many times have you heard an employee say, "I'm working on it? There were a few set-backs out of my control, so it's not completed yet." Usually it's the same people who make these same excuses, over and over. Rarely do you hear them say, "Here it is. It's done!" Even when there are issues beyond one's scope; there are inadequate resources; there is an unreasonable time-line; or, critical information is missing, the trademark of a genuine leader is one who works through barriers and delivers a positive outcome. If you don't have what you need, you don't wait until the due date to present inadequate resources as your justification. What your superiors see is a person who has few deliverables, yet an abundance of excuses. In a quiet moment, take an inventory of your successes versus failures. Be sure to place projects you've labeled as "almost done" in the "failure" column. With your track record in mind, answer honestly, "Would you want you on your team?"

13 *"Tomorrow is often the busiest day of the week."*
— Spanish Proverb

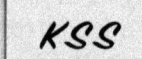

The weakest response one can receive when asking another about a task they have committed to do is "I will do it tomorrow." What they are saying is, "I need to buy more time." We all know and see people who keep putting things off until tomorrow. Tomorrow becomes a warehouse full of excuses. Yet, if we are to take their response seriously, tomorrow will always be the busiest day of the week for them.

Workplace Application

Ahh, the folly of "Workplace Procrastination!" You'll recognize the, "I should have that ready for you tomorrow!" group, although the date of assigned delivery was today! The adage is absolutely true that, "If you want something done, give it to someone who is busy!" There's a reason that these employees are busy. They're occupied delivering outstanding outcomes in the workplace instead of delivering excuses! Faced with workplace overload, they set about evaluating, organizing and executing today, not tomorrow! And the cycle continues as more and more leaders discover they can trust these employees to deliver, even under difficult circumstances. These productive employees are building a reputation for being invaluable to the organization. While the "I'll get it done tomorrow" group is smug, believing that they've learned how to out-maneuver and avoid the excessive overload of their peers, they later discover that the organization allocates rewards in the same manner that others deliver outcomes. Those delivering on-time quality outcomes are assigned their rewards "today," while the wily procrastinators are promised that their rewards are definitely forthcoming – "tomorrow!"

> **14**
>
> *"Things may come to those who wait, but only the things left by those who hustle."*
>
> – Abraham Lincoln

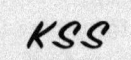

There is someone out there 'waiting in the weeds' for someone else to trip and fall, to flame out, or to give up and move on. Their philosophy is 'stay low and keep moving'. They are the corporate equivalent of bottom feeders, waiting for some crumbs to drop into their sphere. They believe that "Being in the right place at the right time is necessarily beneficial." However, consider that there will always be people who can out talk you, out write you, out-smooze you and, even out think you. You might not be the biggest, brightest, fastest or strongest, but if you are truly ambitious, it does not satisfy you to wait for crumbs to fall. Instead, you're constantly out-hustling, out-working and even out-thinking the competition. If you work smarter, harder, longer, and more diligently than anyone else, you will reap the rewards of your efforts. As my mother used to say, "You can't control the outcome, but you can always control your effort." Manifest in your mind the situation you would like to see materialize. Now, equipped with this vision of a better future state, adopt the attitude of being an "Out-Master" (out-hustling, out-working, and out-thinking the competition).

Workplace
Application

Good things don't come to those who wait. It's up to you to hustle to find, claim or create that which you consider the "good things" in the workplace. If you find that you're always being outraced, outfoxed, or non-preferred, change your race strategy. If the hustlers have once again gained the significant roles, and you are once again claiming the crumbs, do something transformational with the crumbs. Read, study, observe in order to innovate the role using new and leading edge techniques. Be ready to relate how you developed your concept, innovated, and partnered to re-engineer the role. Keep innovating until someone recognizes that you are a phenomenal change agent, the company's turn-around genius.

> *15* "Champions are made from something they have deep inside them, a desire, a dream, a vision... they have to have the skill and the will. But the will must be stronger than the skill."
> – Muhammad Ali

KSS We often think that successful people are endowed with a 'special gift' or are simply just smarter. Yet, the actual difference between successful people and those who are not is drive, desire, and determination. I call the ability to harness these qualities 'willpower'. You may also call this trait 'staying power' or the ability to 'motor on' or 'push through'. While others complain, point fingers, and claim that they didn't get 'a fair chance', the successful person employs 'will power' to win. To be successful, you must go deep inside yourself and issue a challenge to your mind. Will power is based on persistence—the ability to keep on keeping on, and the decision to never give up.

Workplace Application

Examine yourself! If everyone else is getting further ahead in the workplace, maybe everyone else is pursuing success more vigorously while you are spending more time peering and pouting! A half-committed effort or mediocre effort will not get you to the winner's circle. Whether it's talent, work ethic, or sheer will, you've got to give it your all! Assess the level at which you're really contributing consistently, not the "I work my butt off" narrative that you present to others. After a realistic self-examination, dust off your talent, fuel up with willpower and move full speed ahead in all the ways and places you've been slacking.

16

> *"Success is the ability to go from failure to failure without losing your enthusiasm!"*
>
> – Sir Winston Churchill

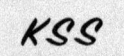

The fear of failure paralyzes most people. Yet, successful people are really just 'successful failures'. While most people would simply give up, successful people realize that failure is the best teacher in the world - they now can start over with more knowledge of what not to do. It's okay to make a mistake! The problem comes about when you make the same mistake repeatedly. So, when you experience a failure, remember that it is nature's way of preparing you for a successful encore.

Workplace Application

When you make a mistake in the workplace, quickly own up to it and explain your rationale for what you did and why. By the way, bring along your thoughts on what you should have done differently. Trying to deny that you made a mistake or making lame excuses for your mistakes will quickly diminish your reputation in the eyes of leaders. Don't allow a mistake to immobilize you. Instead, do a close examination of what went wrong. Get feedback from trusted colleagues (they've already heard about it anyway). Be direct and honest with your boss while asking for feedback. Then make your successful comeback with a well-researched and well-conceived plan to "Make It Work!"

17 "Eighty percent of success is showing up."
– Woody Allen

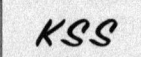

Woody's statement is profound in its simplicity. Couple his observation with old Ben's and you see that 'being in the room' where decisions-making takes place is the key to having a successful career. Even if you're not the sharpest person in the room, you still have a leg up on the person who didn't have the privilege of being in the room. Remember, in this world, there are three types of people: "those who watch things happen; those who make things happen; and those who wonder what happened." If you show up, you will at least know what happened and, perhaps you will even be in the position to make things happen.

Workplace Application

Just as Benjamin Franklin admonished one to "get there" on time, for some, the admonition begins with "just getting there!" Any organization, leader or manager must be able to rely upon their people. Can others count on you? Do you frequently walk in the door to work or into meetings with a long list of excuses regarding why you are late? Do you always have explanations for why the project isn't complete? And, did you realize that "getting there" also refers to getting to the end of a project? If you've created a profile of not getting there on time, or not getting there at all, others will quickly assess that they cannot count on you, and they won't!

18

> "Only when the tide goes out do you discover who has been swimming naked."
>
> – Warren Buffett

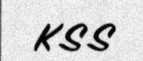

Managing with unlimited resources can make anyone look like a genius. The proper test is managing and leading with scarce resources. During times of surplus, how many times have we watched self-proclaimed visionaries pontificate about the future and the current state of affairs? Yet, when things go south and resources shrink, these "geniuses" also shrink and reveal their nakedness.

Workplace Application

Everyone in the workplace is a genius! They are smarter than their bosses, the leadership and the board of directors. Sitting around during a chat fest, they know exactly what should have been done, what should be done, who should do it, and when they should do it! According to this group, no one in charge is fit for their role, which is why the company is not more successful. But alas, talk is cheap! When the company faces a major hurdle or blunder (which even the best-run companies do), and asks for viable solutions to their business challenges, it is amazing that the most viable suggestions so often come from employees whom leadership has never heard from – or heard of? And where are the perennial pontificators now? These naked geniuses are busily trying to cover themselves by criticizing the brilliant recommendations offered by their well-dressed offenders, those diligent and knowledgeable employees with few words, but with real-life solutions.

19

> *"In the end, we will remember not the words of our enemies, but the silence of our friends."*
> – Dr. Martin Luther King, Jr.

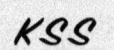

We know who our enemies are and how they feel about us. We are never truly surprised by their hateful words, deeds, or actions. In fact, we brace ourselves for their onslaught. But, we experience the highest form of betrayal when those considered our friends assume the posture of "My name is Bennett and I'm not in it." We do and should expect more from our friends, although we should never expect a friend to bear the entire burden of our life's challenges. Neither do we expect them to disappear and become mute when we need them the most. When under attack, the smallest gesture of support from our friends is a major boost to our psyche, audacity, and willpower.

Workplace Application

If silence speaks volumes, then silence from our friends and supporters speaks a library. However, in the heat of the battle, it is critical not to waste your mental power lamenting the members of your posse who have distanced themselves from you, no matter how tempting! Focus on the issue at hand and seek approaches, strategies and people (although they may be few) who can help you appropriately navigate your circumstances. Find someone neutral to assist you in evaluating your missteps. Take ownership of your mistakes and accept responsibility for resolving them. Seek seasoned professionals, mentors and friends outside the workplace to assist you in strategizing your comeback. However, "fess-up everything" which will allow them the best chance of guiding you appropriately. Amid it all, remember to make no new enemies! And importantly, don't forget to assess which of your "friends" need to be re-labeled as "acquaintances."

20 "Silence is often misinterpreted but never misquoted."
–Author Unknown

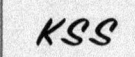

Often times in situations, we feel compelled to say something, regardless of whether our remarks add value. As my father used to tell me, "If you have nothing to say, then say nothing!" Know that silence can be a powerful statement. Your silence can communicate agreement, disagreement, or the need for more information. What you should never forget is that while you have muted your voice, your 'non-verbals' can be awfully loud. While your mouth is closed, your eyes and facial expressions are sending specific messages about how you are truly feeling. Even with 'loud non-verbals' overriding your verbal silence, often silence is still golden.

Workplace Application

Here's a sure-fire formula for motivating eyeballs to roll, furtive glances to be exchanged, mischievous smiles to be flashed and quickly hidden, and deep sighs to be evoked - always have something to say — on everything! It is rare that a single individual is an expert or has general knowledge of every topic. Yet, a chosen few in the workplace feel they must project the image of the all-knowing authority — from rare earth minerals to medieval methods of soap making. They reinforce their own notion of having superior knowledge by educating the less erudite among us. While it may be quite true that these individuals have expertise in more than one area, it is only in their true areas of expertise that they should be the frequent contributors, and "frequent" is not synonymous with "always." If you need to speak on every topic, take a glance at your audience. If your audience suddenly fixate on their cell phones, it's possible that while you are delivering your eloquent views, they are exchanging texts regarding their eloquent views about you.

21

> *"If we're playing for fun, why keep score?"*
>
> – Al McGuire,
> Hall of Fame Basketball Coach

KSS

How many times have you been told, "just kidding" only to find out that someone was keeping track of your missteps? I vividly remember an aspiring basketball player who challenged me to play a one-on-one game. Often the person challenging me would say, "let's play for fun." Invariably, as the game unfolded, the challenger would blurt out the score, if they were winning of course. As soon as they announced the score, I realized that I might have been playing for fun — but the challenger was playing to win. In business settings, others often confront us about something we said or did, humorously, but with a definite sting. Sometimes a boss or peer will pretend that they meant these remarks in jest. These remarks come back to us in formal evaluations of our performance. Remember, there are no "throwaway lines" whether couched in humor or delivered in anger.

Workplace Application

In the workplace, we often play this out as a joke at others' expense, followed by the infamous tagline, "I was just kidding." Actually, the perpetrator is playing a game of one-upmanship, but asking that you refrain from keeping score as they hit home-run after home-run, until the scoreboard reads 21-0. Your score, incidentally, is the 0. In the workplace, you don't have to be in the race to experience others racing against you. So, don't be lulled by the charismatic manner in which the opponent delivers their career blows. "Were just playing for fun" on the playing field is the same as "I was just kidding" in the workplace. Just as they really were keeping score in a "just for fun" ball game, they intended the words that preceded "I was just joking," to deliver a negative career blow. While you should always play to win, "winning" is competing with dignity and grace, even when grace and dignity are not afforded to you. The key is to show no offense, even if the offender is intentionally offensive. If what they said is incorrect or damaging, calmly and firmly correct them on the spot. Work on creating an outwardly calm and unflappable demeanor. Importantly, resist the slippery slope of becoming paranoid. Not every comment is worth your time, and neither is every commentator.

22

> *"Everyone is entitled to his own opinion, but not his own facts."*
> – Daniel Patrick Moynihan, Former US Senator

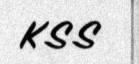

Over the past several years, we have witnessed the emergence of a bogus concept called "alternative facts." In reality, "alternative facts" are simply "lies" attempting to present themselves as facts. Facts are value neutral. Facts don't have agendas. Facts are objective and non-partisan. Today, fact-based arguments are under attack. Outright lying is being normalized. Lying has become so pervasive that a cottage industry of 'fact checkers' has emerged to challenge and dispute blatant lies and embellished statements. So much of the divisiveness that we face today results from the rising tide of lies being spewed hourly by politicians, executives, colleagues and others. Social media has become the breeding ground for "prevaricators" masquerading as "factualists."

Workplace Application

Once you form a habit, it is so difficult to break, thus the proliferation of lying! We start perhaps by telling our parents that we didn't do the dastardly deed at school, and that the teacher lied on us (but we did the deed and are rather proud that our fake sincerity fooled our parents)! Over the years, our lies become so frequent, insidious, and efficacious that they slowly form our moral fabric. Yet lies have consequences, and the workplace is no exception! Lying about workplace achievements will be discovered eventually, and embarrassment and disgrace will be eager to welcome you. Providing a negative, but false, assessment of someone's career potential not only negatively compromises the employee's career, but their well-being and their hopes and dreams - and perhaps even you when others report disparate assessments. Lying about skills that you do not possess can lead to destruction and loss of lives. Consider that completing a maintenance log falsely verifying that a production line, a plane or a car has been serviced, can lead to major destruction. Taking credit for achievements that are not yours will eventually lead to The Peter Principle — rising to the level where you can't fake it anymore! Remember, for every lie told in the workplace, there is someone who suspects or knows the truth. Fact: There are no white lies, minor discrepancies, miscommunications or alternative facts. There are lies, and those who tell them are liars!

23

> "Who is more foolish, the child afraid of the dark or the man afraid of the light?"
>
> —Maurice Freehill

KSS

Adults, too often, forget about their childish fears. We forget that the all-encompassing darkness that enveloped us as children was real. This heavy drape of menacing darkness invoked fears of monsters, ghosts and a host of unknown scary creatures, which caused us to cover our heads with pillow and sheets. Even if we survived one night of darkness, we knew that the fear would return the next night. Our adult fears are no longer fixated on the dark. Rather, as adults, we now fear getting new information that might challenge our view of our daily world. When others challenge our perspectives and beliefs, we metaphorically cover our head and plug our ears. We are afraid of new insights, information and facts that leave us feeling alone and fearful. New insights should bring new light into our thought processes. But for some, it is this new light that exposes our fear of adult darkness.

Workplace Application

One thing we fear most in the workplace is feedback! The lack of feedback is darkness, and the provision of feedback is a glowing light. We should look forward to it, but most often we avoid feedback at all costs! We often fear feedback, although innately we already know how we are performing (whether we are delivering high quality, at rapid pace, through teamwork, without dead bodies strewn throughout the hallways). If our performance is not up to par, we'd rather remain in darkness and complain about our circumstances than receive the knowledge that lights the way to a more successful path. NASA highlights that, "When a rocket in space sends messages to Earth, the signals are received and interpreted by certain mechanisms that then send FEEDBACK to the rocket in order that it can correct its position." It is why feedback is so critically important to employees. If you receive feedback and make the proper adjustments, you can correct your positioning and trajectory. If you are still fearful of receiving feedback, do as Dr. Susan Jeffers advises in her book, "Feel the Fear and Do It Anyway!"

24

> *"Too often we honor swagger and bluster and wielders of force; too often we excuse those who are willing to build their own lives on the shattered dreams of others."*
> *– Robert F. Kennedy*

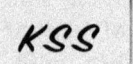

We routinely celebrate bullies, tyrants and unethical business leaders as "successful" because they always seem to get their way. Yet the road they traveled to success is littered with the people they've trampled, exploited, and misused. Their overbearing behavior is a cover for the fears and insecurities that linger deep inside, which they believe will be exposed without proactive steps to keep others at bay. A large part of the problem is that we equate success with material wealth, influence, and power. We are so blinded by the flash of their material possessions that we can't see beyond their posturing and the trinkets and trash that they flash.

Workplace Application

Since by definition and by observation, bullies are nothing more than cowards who get their way by throwing adult temper tantrums - fear not! The best response to take the sound out of their thunder is to remain calm and confident. Maintain a relaxed posture and a pleasant and professional demeanor. If the bully is loud and obnoxious, ask, "What is it that I can help you with?" If they continue with their performance, pleasantly add, "Perhaps we can reconvene at a different time." Then, cover yourself by updating everyone important to the matter. Relate the conversation, the scene and the tone in a non-emotional manner, and ask for guidance. And "Yes," as a professional you will need to follow-up with the bully by sending a meeting request, including only those needed for resolution. And when the bully pulls this stunt again - and they will — repeat the process!

25

> *"Live in such a way that you wouldn't be ashamed to sell the family parrot to the town gossip."*
>
> – Will Rogers

KSS

Too often we live our lives in a way that hides who we really are from neighbors, friends, and strangers. We carefully and meticulously create a persona strictly for public view and consumption. We reserve showing who we really are to our family and very close friends. Often we play out our lack of tolerance, patience and consideration at home. Thus, we have a public persona and a private persona. In fact, the word persona derives from the Latin word for "mask." While we have a public mask, our inner personality is often at variance with our public persona. Our daily challenge is to reconcile this public face with our private face. It is difficult and draining to keep hiding who we really are from the public. Once we stop relying on the public face to hide our prejudices, biases and actually work on these less acceptable behaviors, the town gossip has nothing negative to share about us. Even the family parrot has nothing negative to squawk about to the town gossip. "What you see is what you get. And what you don't see is better yet."

Workplace Application

Just as town gossips develop a negative reputation, so do company gossips. Why does the company gossip have a negative reputation? It is because they can't be trusted! If they give you personal information about someone else, most have discovered that they don't discriminate. They will give others personal information about you! If tempted to share any personal information with the company gossip, they'll assuredly add this new tasty morsel to their ever-increasing repertoire! An old southern adage is, "A dog that will bring a bone, will carry one," meaning if someone will gossip to you, they'll also gossip about you. While you should definitely stay connected enough in the workplace to know what is going on, what jobs may be in the works, who may be leaving —beware of gossip, especially malicious gossip. If we know that a colleague spreads malicious gossip, FLEE from them in the most professional but expeditious way. Why? Because people will correctly assume that "Birds of a feather flock together." Let your professional demeanor and your appropriate distance send the message, "Don't Flock With Me!"

MEET THE CAST

(Pictured from left to right)

Top Row: Reva, Samuel, Brenda, Phil, Maya
Second Row: Lavett, Kwame, Mary, Maharai, Samuel
Bottom Row: Henry, Nealie, James, Evelyn, Albertha

On assignment and missing from the photo are: George, Jerry, Keri, Matt, Terry, Hosea, Grace, Kevin, Matt, Lauren

The Wisdom of Owls

The owl has been used as a symbol of knowledge, wisdom, shrewdness and insight throughout the world for multiple generations. While it is impossible to know exactly which culture first associated the owl with wisdom, many theorize that its use originated from Greek Mythology. Whatever its origin, the owl is used to represent wisdom, truth, intuitive knowledge and patience across western cultures (e.g. Greek, Italian, Celtic, Native American), as well as other cultures including, Japanese, African, and many more.

Why the owl? It is believed that the owl's larger than usual eyes, solemn express, mysterious demeanor gave rise to the its symbolic status. Furthermore, the owl's natural abilities lend credence to this representation. The owl has keen eyesight – being able to see through the dark, incredible patience, the ability to fly almost soundlessly, enhanced auditory reception, and measured and precise movements – abilities most humans desire.

As we have so generously used the owl to symbolize quotes on wisdom for the workplace, it seems only appropriate to leave you with a final quote about the wise owl.

"A wise old owl sat on an oak; The more he saw the less he spoke; The less he spoke the more he heard; Why aren't we like that wise old bird?"

- Unknown

www.ingramcontent.com/pod-product-compliance
Lightning Source LLC
Chambersburg PA
CBHW060857050426
42453CB00008B/1000